Day and Night

written by Maria Gordon
and
illustrated by Mike Gordon

Wayland

Simple Science

Air	Light
Colour	Materials
Day and Night	Push and Pull
Heat	Rocks and Soil
Electricity and Magnetism	Skeletons and Movement
Float and Sink	Sound

Series Editor: Catherine Baxter
Advice given by Audrey Randall – member of the Science Working Group for the National Curriculum.

First published in 1995 by
Wayland (Publishers) Ltd
61 Western Road, Hove
East Sussex, BN3 1JD, England

British Library Cataloguing in Publication Data
Gordon, Maria
  Day and Night. – (Simple Science Series)
  I. Title II. Gordon, Mike III. Series
  525.35

ISBN 0-7502-1295-0

Typeset by MacGuru
Printed and bound in Italy by G Canale and C.S.p.A., Turin, Italy

Contents

It is day when the Sun lights up
the world around you.

It is night when the world around
you is dark.

Days are light because the Sun shines very brightly. There is no sunshine at night, so nights are dark. Most people and many animals and plants are busy in the day and rest at night.

Other animals and plants are busy at night. They are nocturnal. Nocturnal animals can see with very little light or they use other ways to tell what is around them.

Which nocturnal animals can you see here?

Animals like tiny shellfish and fireflies make their own light at night so they can find each other!

Some plants, like honeysuckle, have flowers which smell stronger at night. Moths come to feed on them.

Long ago, people saw how the Sun gives light to the Earth. Some used huge stones to make patterns for the Sun to shine through. Many thought the Sun was a god. They gave the Sun names like Apollo, Ra and Surya.

People gave names to stars and planets too. They learnt that they could see different stars from different places. This helped them to find their way on long journeys.

The Earth is like a giant ball in space. The Sun looks smaller, but really it is a much bigger ball that is very far away. The Moon really is smaller than the Earth but it is much closer than the Sun.

Sun

Moon

earth

This is how the Earth, Moon and Sun would look if you saw them from a flying saucer.

Look out of a window at different times of day. The Sun seems to move across the sky. Ask a grown-up to help you make a chart showing how the Sun seems to move.

10 o'clock

12 O'clock

2 O'clock

9 o'clock

4 O'clock

7 o'clock

6 O'clock

Do this on Summer and Winter days. The Sun seems lower in Winter.

Really the Earth is moving, not the Sun!
People used to think the Sun moves around
the Earth. But scientists called
Aristarchus, Copernicus and
Galileo showed that the Earth
moves around the Sun.

Galileo proved it when
telescopes were invented.

The Earth takes a year to go round the Sun. But the Earth also spins slowly while it goes round.

Ask a grown-up to help you push a pencil through the middle of an orange. Turn the pencil to make the orange spin. This is how the Earth turns while it moves through space.

Ask a grown-up to put a lamp without a shade in the middle of a table. Switch on the light. (Don't look straight at the bulb.)

Put a red sticker on one side of the orange and a green sticker on the other. Spin the orange slowly on the edge of the table. First one sticker is lit up, then the other.

The stickers on your orange are like places on different sides of the world. As the Earth turns, the Sun shines on the places on one side. It is day in these places.

The places on the other side of the Earth are turned away from the Sun. There, it is night.

As the Earth keeps turning, the dark places come back into the light. People there can see the Sun very low down in the sky. This is called sunrise. It is the beginning of the day.

The Earth keeps turning so the Sun seems
to get higher. The time when the Sun is
highest in the sky is the middle of the
day. This is called noon.

The Earth carries on turning. The daytime places are slowly turned away from the Sun. The Sun seems to get lower. Then it cannot be seen any more. This is called sunset. It is the end of day and the beginning of night.

Make your orange and pencil lean like this. This is how the Earth leans! This means parts of the Earth are closer to the Sun than others. These places take longer to turn away from the Sun so their days are longer.

The places at the other end of the world are further away from the Sun. These places have very long nights.

How long are your days?

Was the Sun in the sky
before you got up?

What will you be
doing after sunset?

What time of year is it?

Ask a grown-up to help you make charts showing how long days last in Winter, Spring, Summer and Autumn. Winter days are shortest. Winter is the time when a place is furthest from the Sun. This is because the Earth is leaning.

Day is the time between sunrise and sunset.
But day is also the name for a whole day
and night together!
Spin your orange and pencil once so the
stickers end up where they started.
This is like the Earth turning once.
The time it takes is called a day.

How many days is it to your birthday? The answer tells you how many times the Earth will turn until that time.

You cannot feel the Earth turning. It feels as if the Earth is still and the Sun is moving around the Earth.

Unlike the Sun, the Moon really does move round the Earth. It takes twenty nine and a half days to go right round. You can see it best at night.

The Moon looks as if it is shining, but it cannot make its own light. It is lit up by the Sun. When the Earth is between the Sun and the Moon, it stops some of the light, so only part of the Moon is lit up.

This is why the Moon seems to change shape.

People use light to help them work and play. Light makes your eyes work. This is how you know it is day. Blind people's eyes do not work. They use special clocks to tell them when it is day or night.

Notes for adults

The 'Simple Science' series helps children to reach Key Stage 1: Attainment Targets 1-4 of the Science National Curriculum.
Below are some suggestions to help complement and extend the learning in this book.

4/5 Where is the sun on cloudy days? Make day and night sky montages. Define the sun as a star.

6/7 Take the same walk at night and in the daytime. Compare land and sea at night. Investigate bioluminescent algae and plankton. Note changes and the use of different senses. Talk about shift workers. Write about sleep and dreams.

8/9 Visit a planetarium and an Egyptian museum exhibit. Investigate Stonehenge. Make a multicultural display featuring artefacts relating to the Sun and sun-gods. Find current depictions of the Sun, the Moon and stars. Make your own. Read the story of Icarus. Borrow a sextant. Use a sundial.

10/11 Make a display of photographs taken in space. Make a giant bar-chart showing comparative sizes of the Sun, the Moon and the Earth.

12/13 Use telescopes and binoculars. Give and explain safety warnings about looking at the Sun. Research the scientists mentioned (note they are men and compare modern role of women in science). Investigate the Hubble telescope.

14/15 Display and mark off different styles of calendars. Compare those from different cultures, eg Chinese. Explain leap years. Look at old scientific models of orbiting planets.

16/17 Communicate with someone in a country in a different time zone.

	Show dateline and time zones on maps and globes.
18/19	Plot temperatures throughout a sunny day. Watch a sunset.
20/21	Investigate six-month-long nights and days in the Arctic and Antarctica. Compare temperatures – south is colder – and relate to tilt of Earth. Research lives of indigenous peoples, such as Laplanders and Inuits.
22/23	Make pie-charts showing activities throughout twenty-four hours. Compare charts made in different seasons.
24/25	Spin a globe to show how the earth turns during a day.
26/27	Read stories about the Moon such as the Ashanti tribe's story of Anansi, Chinese tales of sun sisters and moon brothers and native American legends of the sun-stealing coyote. Investigate tides.
28/29	Watch films made with infra-red light. Go badger, worm, slug and hedgehog watching at night. Use glow-in-the-dark stickers to demonstrate phosphorescence. Stay up till midnight!

Other books to read

Day and Night by K. Davies and W. Oldfield (Wayland, 1992)
Light by R. Chase (Blackwell Education, 1990)
Poems about Day and Night selected by A. Earl and
D. Sensier (Wayland, 1995)
Sight by M. Suhr (Wayland, 1993)

Index